£ 1·50

The Saint annual

Contents

The Girl in the Boot	6
Round the World – Quiz	15
A Packet of Trouble	18
Crossword	26
Lady Helen's Necklace	28
Roberts Return	36
What do you know about the Saint?	42
Leslie Charteris and the Stick Man	43
The Saint Leads a Dance	44
The Saint Drives a Jaguar	52
All You Need is a Good Agent	54
The Saint at Home	60
Answers	61

Stafford Pemberton Publishing

Copyright © MCMLXXVIII by Leslie Charteris
Based on 'Return of the Saint' an
ITV Production
All rights reserved throughout the world.
Published in Great Britain by Stafford Pemberton
Publishing Co. Ltd., The Ruskin Chambers,
Drury Lane, Knutsford, Cheshire WA16 6HA.
Printed in Italy.
ISBN 0 86030 138 9.

A GIRL IN THE BOOT

THE SAINT, Simon Templar, was driving along a winding road whistling carelessly. He loved driving fast cars, but better still he loved to watch the professionals handle their machines round tight bends in all sorts of weather. Also motor racing seemed to attract the most beautiful women spectators, and where there were beautiful women, there was the Saint.

He had been speeding along behind a Mercedes quite content to follow at a mere 90 mph. Suddenly the road dipped and narrowed. They had come to a little parade of small shops.

The Mercedes slowed down and stopped. The Saint knew he couldn't get past the Mercedes because it hadn't pulled in far enough to the curb and was blocking the road so he stopped some yards back.

The driver of the Mercedes jumped out and ran into one of the shops leaving the engine running. No sooner had the man disappeared into the shop than a sharp faced youth, who had been lounging against a building, jumped into the Mercedes pulled the door to and put his foot on the accelerator. With a roar of its

engine the Mercedes swung away.

The driver ran out of the shop shouting at the retreating car. The Saint's car purred up to the angry man.

"Get in" he ordered. "Let's see if we can catch him."

The driver looked at the Saint and saw a keen tanned face and very clear blue eyes that danced with mischief. "Naughty, naughty," said the Saint. "You should never leave a car unattended with its engine running."

"But it was only for a second," stammered the driver.

"Famous last words. But we'll soon put that right." The Saint's Jaguar XJS picked up speed and began to eat up the distance between itself and the Mercedes. At 90 mph the two cars careered along the Riviera seafront. The Mercedes was swinging violently from side to side, weaving about as if trying to shake itself free of its followers.

"That fool. Look at the way he's treating a perfect engine," shouted the Saint's companion. "If he knew how to drive he would leave us standing."

"Do I take that as an insult to the way I handle this car?" asked the Saint.

"No. No. You are a very good driver. But that Mercedes has a new invention. In any international race it would be a winner."

"Really! how very interesting," said the Saint softly.

He was catching up with the stolen car now. Gradually he eased alongside and slowly forced the Mercedes to pull to one side.

"Careful," cried his passenger in anguish," please be careful. Do not harm the car."

"Don't worry, old sport. I know what I'm doing."

The youth in the Mercedes realised that he was losing the battle. He skidded

to a halt jumped out and ran off.

The Saint braked hard and the XJS jolted to a standstill. "Right, let's get after him."

"No leave him. He is not important."

"Oh well," the Saint shrugged, "if you insist." He was just about to get back into his car when he heard a violent knocking on the boot of the Mercedes.

His companion ran to the back of the car and opened the boot. A beautiful brunette crawled out, painfully. Her eyes blazed as she advanced on the man. "What sort of driving do you call that Mario?"

"But my love . . ." Mario parried her blows.

"Don't my love me. I am black and blue all over from your terrible driving."

"But it wasn't me driving, my beautiful one."

"Have you gone mad? Of course you were driving."

"No. No. Someone took the car when I got out to buy cigarettes and this man helped me give chase."

"Oh!" she gasped and stared at the two men.

"I know it's none of my business," said the Saint gently, "but do you always travel in the boot of a car?"

"We are not doing anything wrong," she said defiantly. "But Mario and I, we have to be careful how we meet. My name is Mariella Bienzi."

"Now I recognise your face," said the Saint. "Your photographs do not do you justice. Suppose we drive to the nearest café and you can tell me what this is all about."

Mario and Mariella got into the Mercedes and drove off. The Saint drove his Jaguar after them. He was half expecting them to speed away, but they slowed down and stopped at a small bar perched on top of a cliff. The view over the Mediterranean was breathtaking. "We always stop here," Mariella told the Saint. "They know us and we can trust them."

They ordered long cool drinks and strolled on to the terrace to admire the view. "Salut!" said the Saint holding up his glass. "You are Mario Lamberto, car designer, your reputation is well known."

"You have heard of me then?"

"I hear of everyone who is noteworthy, dear boy. I heard that you'd been sacked from the Calvani racing team for some unmentionable crime. I must say I thought it odd at the time."

"That crime was to fall in love with me," burst in Mariella. "Of all the unfair, treacherous, loathsome things my guardian did. It makes me angry that that man controls all my money. I am a pauper if he says so."

"But you are rich are you not?" asked the Saint puzzled.

"My mother and father were killed in an air crash. Signor Calvani is a distant relative. My father made him my guardian and I cannot marry without his consent. And I cannot have my money until I marry. Mario and I love each other. When Calvani found out he sacked Mario on some trumped up charge."

"But you were his chief designer."

"I was for many years. All his victorious cars have been my models. Calvani told me there was no need for contracts between friends. Always I was promised a share of the profits, but I never got them. So I refused to give him my new invention without a contract and he sacked me. Now I am out on the street. How can I marry Mariella with no job?"

The Saint put down his drink and stood up, gazing out over the Mediterranean. "You say you have a new engine in the Mercedes now?"

"Yes, it is revolutionary. According to my experiments no other car will beat it, providing it is driven by an expert. But of course I cannot enter it in any race now," Mario hid his head in his hands.

"How about Roger Knight giving it a try?" the Saint asked.

"Roger Knight," echoed Mario. "But he's the world champion."

"He's had a row with his team manager who'd promised him a new car and hasn't come up with one, so now he's out on a limb."

"But do you think he'd be interested?"
"He would, if I asked him," said the Saint. "Let me know where I can contact

you. In the meantime wouldn't it be much more comfortable for Mariella to sit in the front seat of my car than in the boot of yours?"

Mario looked doubtful.

"Trust me, my friend," said the Saint. "Leave it to me and you will be married soon, Mariella will get her fortune, and you will get enough to start your own racing team."

In less than an hour the Saint was driving through the gates of Calvani's mansion, and past the guard.

"See that man," Mariella nudged the Saint's arm. "He will be phoning my guardian to tell him I am with a man."

"Disgraceful, isn't it?"

The drive was a long one up to the large house. When they arrived Signor Calvani was waiting on the steps of his house. "Mariella what is this? Why are you not resting?"

"Because I was showing Mr. Templar the sights," she said defiantly. "This is Mr. Simon Templar."

The Saint extended a languid hand and put on an aristocratic voice. "Nice to meet you, Senior Calvani. Came over for the racing. Got a new motor. Jolly fast. Roger Knight's driving it. Says nothing will touch it."

Calvani studied the Saint for several minutes. "Please come inside," he said.

"Oh I say, jolly nice of you and all that." He followed his host inside, through a large hall with a marble floor out into a sun lounge which overlooked a terraced garden.

"May I offer you some refreshment."

"You got any whisky, old chap?"

Calvani poured him out a stiff one. "Tell me about your car."

"Oh very hush hush. Got a secret engine. Moves along at tremendous speed. Designed it myself. Had enormous offers for it, simply enormous. Don't need the money. Well, I might sell it for a beautiful brunette," he turned and winked at Mariella.

Calvani took the Saint's glass and filled it with an even larger whisky. The Saint took it and downed it in one gulp.

10

"Beautiful girl, she your daughter?"

"No Mr. Templar. I am her guardian."

"Lucky you. Wish I was her guardian, don't you know. Well, old thing," he took Mariella's hand and kissed it. "How about coming to watch the trials. Seeing Roger tonight. Must tell him about you."

"Perhaps you will permit me to come to watch," Calvani escorted the Saint to the door. "I would bring Mariella of course."

"Anything you say, squire. Expect you at the track tomorrow afternoon. Bye." The Saint got into his car and drove off down the drive.

No sooner had Calvani seen the Saint down the drive than he jammed down several buttons on the intercom. "Jake, Ross, Blake, follow that silly ass Englishman and stick with him."

Three heavyweight, thick set men ran out of the lodge by the gate and jumped into a car. They drove through the gates and down the road a short distance and then parked in a side turning.

The Saint noticed them as he drove by. "There you are my fine friends. I thought I'd have company before long." He drove at a friendly pace back to the Plaza hotel, parked in the front, gave his keys to the front porter and went inside.

The car behind drove into the car park and waited.

The Saint ran out through the kitchens at the back of the Hotel to Mario who was waiting in the Mercedes.

"Where are we going?" asked Mario.

"To meet Roger of course."

The three men in the car park waited several hours until the telephone in their car buzzed. Calvani's voice shouted down the line. "What are you doing?"

"Nothing, just waiting sir."

"No sign of any development?"

"No sir."

"Well come back. We must make plans. I have work for you to do."

The following afternoon the Saint and Roger Knight were at the track. Knight

was at the wheel of the Mercedes.

"You get all the gen from Mario last night?" asked the Saint.

"Yes, and we had a trial run this morning. Runs really sweet, fast as a cheetah, nothing'll touch us. I've been in hundreds of cars Simon, but never one like this."

"Hallo, Hallo, we've got visitors."

Calvani and Mariella had driven up and were getting out of the car. But the Saint wasn't watching them. He had his eyes on a car that was stationary at the other end of the track.

"I think you're going to be kidnapped," he told Roger.

"I say, steady on."

"It's O.K. I've got it under control. When you've finished the trial come back here and we'll make a switch of the car and the driver."

"What is this all about?"

"Later, old chum, later."

Mario's Mercedes raced off with Roger at the wheel. Shooting round the track the car went at an unbelievable speed.

"What did I tell you," the Saint patted Calvani on the shoulder. "Some speedster what?"

"You certainly seem to have a winner Mr. Templar. Let's hope nothing happens to stop you winning with it."

"Oh, I say. Don't let's be pessimistic."

"Many a slip, you know Mr. Templar, as you English say," Calvani took Mariella's arm and marched her away to the car.

"Right then," said the Saint as Roger drew the Mercedes up beside him. "You wait here until you hear from me."

"But where are you going?"

"I'm going to meet the boys down there, in my borrowed Mercedes."

"But will you be all right?"

"I don't think they'll bother me much."

The Saint drove off at speed towards the waiting car. The three men had parked across the road as a block and signalled the Saint to stop. Instead Simon put his foot on the accelerator and drove straight at them, scattering them in the road. Then he stopped, jammed on the brake, turned, tyres screeching, and came back at them again. This time he hit the car side on and it plummeted over the side of the bank.

By the time the men had recovered enough to reach for their guns the Saint was far away once more. He raced back to Roger waiting at the track. "O.K. so far," he said. "Now I'm going to pay a visit to Calvani. Want to come?"

"Not if there's going to be any rough stuff."

"I'll be as sweet as sugar, you'll see. But that man's got a bill to settle with Mario and I'm going to see he pays it in full."

The Saint drove Roger in the Mercedes up the drive. The man at the gate reported to Calvani and he was at the

door waiting with a slight frown on his face. The Saint got out.

"You'd better send a relief party for your three men down the road. They got a bit tangled up with my other car. Mind if I come inside?" The Saint didn't wait for an answer, just pushed past inside the house.

Mariella was waiting in the sun lounge. Calvani followed the Saint.

"If you wanted my car so badly why didn't you ask," said the Saint gently to Calvani.

"You said you wouldn't sell it to anyone!" Calvani snapped.

"Ah but remember what I did say."

"You mean Mariella?" said Calvani astonished.

Mariella let out a cry. "Simon, you wouldn't . . ." But before she could say any more Simon turned on her and from the look on his face she knew she must keep silent.

"You badly need to win this race, Calvani. In fact you can't afford not to win, hence the episode with your three henchmen. You can't bear to think of all those orders going elsewhere."

"It's true, what you say. Name your price and if you want Mariella, then she's yours."

"I want a letter giving your permission for Mariella to marry the designer of the car . . ."

"That's you," interrupted Calvani.

The Saint didn't answer but continued ". . . and £100,000 for the design outright."

"You drive a hard bargain," muttered Calvani.

"I'll take the letter now," said the Saint.

Calvani went to the desk and hurriedly wrote the note. "Here, take Mariella with my blessing. Mariella go with Mr. Templar."

Mariella, her face buried in a handkerchief left the room followed by the Saint. Once outside the house and in the courtyard she burst into laughter. "Oh dear, he will be furious when he finds out."

"But then it will be too late and when Roger wins, you have Mario and your money and Calvani has his car – fair trade, wouldn't you say?"

She threw her arms round his neck and kissed him, and for just a moment the Saint wished that the letter really did mean him.

Round the World Quiz

The Saint spends much of his time flying off to other countries and of course he knows the right places to go as well as all the facts about the places he visits. How much do you know about other countries? Here is your chance to test your knowledge with a few simple questions, if you don't find them all quite so simple the answers are on page 61.

1. Which city has a tower that looks as if it is about to topple over and which country is it in?

2. You might think you know this one, but are you sure . . . what is the capital of the United States of America?

3. A number of countries have a railway system that runs underground, what is the French system called?

4. A bustling city that has no cars or buses, indeed no roads. Which city is it?

5. You should be able to guess from the name, which country is Mount Fuji in?

6. A rickshaw is a passenger-carrying, man-drawn vehicle . . where might you expect to see it.

7. Which country is known as the land of the midnight sun?

8. In which country would you find the city of Omsk?

9. Where, which country that is, do people eat birds nests for dinner?

10. Aborigines are the natives of which country?

The Saint

THE SAINT IS CALLED IN TO HELP...

21

22

24

CROSSWORD

CLUES

Down

1. Where there's sure to be fire
2. Forbid
3. In the . . .
4. Robbery is one
5. Kojak has none, the Saint has
8. Post it
9. Fast car
10. Simon Templar
11. One who steals
15. Large town
16. Smile when you're -----
17. The Saint sometimes needs to be
19. String of . . . . .
22. Of good character
23. Shave off
25. Needs a hammer
27. Don't get into this
30. The Saint brings crooks into the . . . .
34. What your brain is for
36. To power an engineless boat.

Across

1. Opposite to buy
2. A detective needs to be on it to kick it
4. A noisy break
6. On the finger
7. Before you fire
10. First half of a Saint's name
11. Second half of 10
12. Afternoon drink
13. On the ladder
14. Might have pearls on it
16. Name for property when its stolen
18. Useful when climbing
20. We breathe it in
21. Time for tears or call for help
23. Matched
24. Evening food
26. Divided parts of the loot
28. Left after fire
29. Faith . . and Charity
31. Hands and knees
32. Search or use it for hair
33. Not love
35. What a policeman pounds
37. Take a -----
38. A trap needs it, to lure
39. Used for repairs
40. Part of the chain

Lady Helen's Necklace

Lady Helen Fawcett was stately and aristocratic. She had been a true daughter of the Empire. In her prime she could be seen at Durbahs in India, on Safari in Africa, in Government House in Australia and holding the fort on Gibraltar. She had lived in many large mansions standing in acres of land. Her last residence had been in Eaton Square where she had lived in style supported by many servants.

But now a widow and with a dwindling income, Lady Helen had moved to a mews near the square, not large enough for servants as well. Hence the arrival early every morning of a cheerful daily who cleaned and cooked and was put upon to run errands and do the ironing and all sorts of odd jobs for which she was not paid.

The daily finished at lunch time which left Lady Helen alone to cope with any disasters that may befall her. But as you may imagine Lady Helen was not one to sit about waiting for help. She always kept an eye open for any likely looking male, half her age, to whom she could boom, in her large voice, for help.

It happened that Simon Templar lived in the mews right opposite Lady Helen and she had taken note of this. The first time a fuse blew in the late afternoon, over she went and rang his bell. Luckily for her he was in and over he went to see if he could repair the damage.

After that she would invite him in for drinks and they became good neighbours if not firm friends. However he did begin to notice after months had gone by that one or two valuable items of china began to disappear from her lounge. He said nothing at first, but when he saw his favourite porcelain shepherdess was missing he had to ask what had happened to it.

"My dear boy, needs must when the devil drives. Bills have to be paid. Money is fast ebbing away. I suppose

everything will go in the end, and after all, there is no-one to leave it to. Except the emeralds of course."

"Emeralds?" the Saint pricked up his ears.

"Haven't I told you about them. A gift from a sultan. Of course my husband never knew. A slight indiscretion on my part. But then I was young." she sighed.

The Saint gazed at her in astonishment. It had never occurred to him that she was once young.

"Let me show them to you." She went to the bureau, unlocked it, took out a small strong box and unlocked that. She bought the emerald necklace to show him. It was a beautiful piece of jewellery. The stones shone clear, each one heart shaped, the smaller ones at the back, then growing larger and larger until there was a huge great green heart in the centre front.

Simon whistled. "You really ought to keep that at the bank."

"And have it stolen there. No thank you. No-one knows it's here except you now, and my daily who I would trust with my life." She put the necklace away and locked the desk. "Incidentally I forgot to tell you, the old Rolls is due back next week, if you would care to borrow it at any time."

"I'd love to take it for a spin when I get back from Verona," the Saint told her. "I'm staying with friends for a month. You take care of those emeralds and I'll see you on my return."

Normally the Saint would have worried about those stones but he was so busy in Verona dealing with a couple of international crooks he forgot all about them.

He flew back early one morning and took a taxi to the mews. While he was paying the driver he noticed a uniformed chauffeur in the opposite garage cleaning Lady Helen's old Rolls. The Saint

studied the man carefully. "I know that face. Good Lord, Harry Hawk, what the devil?"

As if he was aware of the Saint's scrutiny the man looked up and saw the Saint. He dropped his leather and walked quickly away, gaining pace as he went and, turning out of the end of the mews he began to run.

"I can see I owe Lady Helen a visit," Simon told himself as he let himself into his house.

One hour and a breakfast later, armed with a large bottle of expensive perfume, the Saint knocked at Lady Helen's front door.

The daily opened it: "Oh sir, nice to see you back. Lady Helen is up and about. Please go in."

The Saint carried in his present and was suitably purred upon while his hostess opened it. She gave a cry of delight and was about to embrace him, but he sidestepped and missed that pleasure.

"Have you taken on a new chauffeur?"

"Yes indeed. Such a nice man. One of nature's gentlemen you might call him."

"How did you get to know of him."

"He came with the Rolls, delivered it for the company. Had impeccable references; the Duke of Radleigh and Lord Monlithe."

"May I see them?"

"Of course, dear boy. Why are you so interested?" She handed the Saint two pieces of notepaper.

The Saint smiled cynically. "Notepaper's O.K. probably stolen. References are forged."

Lady Helen gasped. "What are you saying?"

"That chauffeur of yours was Harry Hawk. He handles stolen jewellery for the big syndicates."

With wide eyes Lady Helen stared at him.

"Will you see if your emeralds are still there?"

She went to the bureau, opened the strong box and lifted out the necklace. She sighed with relief. "Oh you did frighten me for a moment."

"May I?" asked the Saint, holding out his hand for the necklace.

She handed over the necklace. He studied it carefully and shook his head sorrowfully at her. "This isn't yours, Lady Helen. It's a magnificent copy, but I'll stake my life it's not real."

"But how can you tell?"

"The clasp of the original had 15 perfect tiny diamonds. This has 15 tiny diamonds but two aren't perfect. Would you allow me to take this to a friend of mine who is far more expert than I am?"

"Of course. Should I call the police?"

"Not yet. I may be able to lay my hands on your original if you'll give me a few days."

The Saint left Lady Helen pouring herself a stiff brandy and went to find Julius Freeman of Hatton Garden. He and Julius had been at school together and remained firm friends, though Julius had stayed put in his father's diamond firm while the Saint had travelled the world.

Julius was bidding goodbye to a customer at the door of his showroom when the Saint arrived. "Good Heavens, Simon. I didn't think you ever saw the light of day this early, but it is good to see you."

Once inside the Saint came straight to the point. He handed over the necklace to Julius. "True or false?" he asked.

Julius took out his eyeglass and put it to his eye. "Marvellous," he said. "Brilliant. There is only one man who could do that . . ."

He was interrupted by the door opening suddenly and a pretty young girl coming in quickly. "Julius, have you seen my father?"

"No my dear Paula, I haven't. What is more he didn't come for his weekly game of chess last night."

"Oh dear. I can't think what has happened. I've been away for a holiday and there is no sign of him. Do you think I should phone the police?"

"Give it a little time. He is probably out and will be returning home soon."

She nodded, near to tears and left the showroom.

"As I was saying," Julius continued. "The only man who could do that copy would be that girl's father. Hey where are you going?"

"After her." Simon took back the necklace. "Thanks Julius," and with a wave he was on to the street and in his

31

XJS in pursuit of the young lady.

But suddenly he slowed down because he saw that others were interested in following her as well. A large black sedan was slowly keeping up with her and as she reached her apartment block, one of the men inside the car got out and said something to her. She turned and nodded her head. The man again said something and pointed to the car. She followed him and got in.

The black sedan began to gather speed and Simon decided to follow. He had recognised the man who spoke to the girl as one of Harry Hawk's associates and he wasn't sure that the girl should be keeping such company.

The black sedan drove along the embankment, crossed Chelsea Bridge, out through the suburbs, through Purley and on to the main Eastbourne road,

on and on, quite an hour's journey. Suddenly it turned off into a hidden side lane which wound its way up around the hill. The car turned into a drive on the left at the top. On the right was a boarding kennels for dogs and cats.

The Saint swung in here and chatted up the owner about boarding his non-existent dog. She took him round her vast grounds. "We're all alone here, and the dogs have lots of walks. You can walk right round that house next door."

"Can I?" said the Saint suddenly interested. "I think I would like that to stretch my legs. Do you mind?"

"Not at all. You can leave the car in the drive. It'll be quite safe."

The Saint strode off down the lane. Through a break in the trees he could see the back of the house which seemed to have a small L-shaped annexe added to the original structure. He could see

two men leading the young girl into this annexe.

He watched and about two minutes later the two men left, locking the door from the outside. They walked away and disappeared round the front of the house. He walked a bit further on and found a gap in the fence. He climbed through and nonchalantly walked over the garden, but no-one came near. He looked through the window of the annexe and saw the girl with her arms round an old man who was sitting on a stool at a work bench with his head in his hands.

The Saint tapped at the window and the girl looked up startled.

The Saint put his fingers to his lips. He took out a knife and began quietly chipping away at the framework. Then he tapped gently against the glass and it fell in with a tinkle.

"What ho!" he said putting in his hand and opening the other window. With a quick leap he was up on the sill and into the room. "I'm a friend of Julius Freeman. He sent me to bring you back," he said to the old man.

"But you don't understand," whispered Paula's father.

"I do know exactly what's been going on, my friend. And I'm going to put it right. But first you've got to get out of here and pronto." He helped them both out of the window and down the garden to the fence. "You go right back to the good lady at the kennels, tell her you are with me and stay there until I come for you."

The Saint ran quickly back and into the annexe.

"Now one of you ruffians should be back any minute to guard your guests, and I'm ready for you."

Sure enough one of the men who really should have stayed behind to guard the girl and her father, but for the call of

nature, returned and unlocked the door.

"Now then," he said as he came through the door, "if you're good I'll bring you something to eat."

"How kind," said the Saint and leaping forward knocked him out with one blow.

The man shot back as if he'd been hit by a rocket, hit the door and slumped in a heap to the floor.

"You shouldn't come round for a few hours." said the Saint, as he tied the man's legs securely and put a handkerchief gag in his mouth. He dragged the man to the work bench and dumped him underneath it.

"Now for the others!" he said.

He left the annexe and made for the front of the house. He was just about to turn the corner when he saw another car drive up and stop. Hidden by the wall he waited to see who would get out.

A uniformed chauffeur opened the door. "Harry Hawk, of course. I might have known," said the Saint to himself.

"Sorry boss, only joking."

The man called Jack helped Harry carry the passenger on to the wheel chair. Both Sammy Johnson's legs were in plaster.

"Good Lord!" thought the Saint. "Someone must have done it for him inside and that's why they let him out."

"Easy" cried the invalid. "Try to make it look as if I'm a cripple. Don't throw me about like a crate of bananas."

They wheeled the man inside.

"Right," said Sam's voice from the house. "Now we'll do it once more and this time go carefully."

They put him back in the car and took him out again and wheeled him into the

Harry walked to the back door of the car and opened it. He took out a wheel chair and opened it. Then he turned his attention to the occupant of the back seat.

"No! No!" said an educated voice from inside the car. "I want it rehearsed properly. Fetch one of the boys."

For a moment the Saint was puzzled. "I know that voice, but I thought he was in gaol. Sammy Johnson. He must be out on parole."

There was a sound of argument from inside the house and Harry came out with another man. "I tell you Jack, the boss wants a rehearsal proper before we take him to the airport."

"But we've done it over and over," said Jack crossly. "What's this then, stage fright?"

"You do what you're told Jack, otherwise I count you out." an icy voice broke up the argument.

house.

"That's better, and remember, that's how I want it done when you take me to the plane. I'll just get this clobber off and we can go over the plan once more. Leave the door. Frank should be here any minute."

The Saint listened to make sure that all of them had gone right into the house then he came to the front door. There was a dim light in the hall because it was windowless but the Saint could make out the shape of the wheel chair and on the seat were the two plaster casts which the man had had on his legs.

The Saint smiled cynically. He picked up a cast and felt inside. Nestling in a pocket was something hard. He lifted it out and smiled happily. Then he put his hand in his own pocket and transferred the forged necklace into the cast. "I'd like to see Sammy's face when they tell him he's got the wrong one."

The Saint took out a piece of chalk from his pocket. He drew a little figure and a halo, which was his trademark, on the seat and left in a hurry.

On the drive back to town with Paula and her father the old man told how the crooks had kidnapped him and threatened to hurt his daughter if he didn't make a copy of the emerald necklace.

"What will happen to me when the police find out?" he gasped "Will I go to prison?"

"Don't worry my friend. The police won't come into this. There has been no robbery." He held up the real necklace and the old man cried out in astonishment.

"But how did you come by it?"

"That's my story and you don't know anything about it. And believe me you won't hear any more from those people, I've seen to that. I have left my mark

and they won't draw swords with The Saint."

"How can we ever thank you?" whispered the young girl.

"Can you cook?" asked the Saint.

"She is an excellent cook. She learnt in France" said the old man.

Simon turned to Paula.

"I want to give an old lady a celebration dinner in my house. Perhaps you would care to come and help, and bring your father too."

Needless to say the food and wine and the return of the necklace were almost too much for Lady Helen, but with the Saint's help she did manage to stagger home to bed a happier woman.

ROBERTS RETURN

THE PARKER FAMILY HAVE LIVED A LIFE OF LUXURY ON THEIR ESTATE SINCE HENRY'S TWIN ROBERT WAS REPORTED KILLED IN KOREA AND HENRY INHERITED ALL THE FAMILY FORTUNE.... NOW READ ON—

DINNER AT THE PARKERS HENRY, HIS SON JULIAN AND HIS WIFE ARE JOINED BY VIVIENNE, HENRY'S SISTER AND HER HENPECKED HUSBAND.

A TELEGRAM SIR

THANK YOU HAWKES, SMARTEN UP MAN. YOU'RE GETTING PAST IT.

HENRY-IT'S TIME HAWKES WAS PUT TO GRASS!

GOOD GRIEF! ITS FROM ROBERT ALIVE AND KICKING AND HE'S COMING HOME!

IT CAN'T BE... ROBERT'S DEAD

WHAT DOES IT MEAN FATHER!

IT MEANS RUIN FOR ME AND YOU JULIAN!

NEXT DAY

CAN NOTHING BE DONE ABOUT IT?

UNCLE ROBERT I'M YOUR NEPHEW JULIAN

GLAD TO MEET YOU JULIAN

NOT UNLESS ROBERT DOESN'T ARRIVE

SIMON IS INVITED TO A DINNER PARTY AT THE PARKERS. HE IS GREETED BY HAWKES....

41

SAINT QUIZ

1. An actor now well known for playing a character who is licensed to kill, used to play Simon Templar a few years ago. What is his name?

2. The Saint television show is based on a series of books. Do you know the name of the author of the books?

What do you know about the Saint? Try to answer these four questions, you might know all the answers but if not you will find them on page 61.

3. What car does the current Simon Templar drive? The exact model please.

4. What is the name of the actor who now plays the Saint? Now that's easy isn't it?

LESLIE CHARTERIES

Leslie Charteris is one of the world's greatest story-tellers.

He was born in Singapore, the son of a surgeon. By the time he was seven, he was interested in writing and by the age of twelve his parents had taken him around the world several times.

Sent to school in England, he then studied at Cambridge University. Throughout those days, short stories flowed from his pen and he made his first sale, at the age of 16, to the Sovereign Magazine with a story entitled "One Crowded Hour". Written under the pseudonym of Leslie C. Bowyer (Bowyer being his mother's maiden name), the story was set in the Pacific.

He left Cambridge, defying his parents, to take up a full-time writing career in 1926, and his first novel, "X Esquire", was published the following year. It was followed by "The White Rider" and then "Meet the Tiger", which introduced the Saint for the first time. He has been writing about the Saint ever since, and some of his earlier stories with other heroes were rewritten to turn them into the Saint.

A steady output of stories didn't necessarily bring immediate wealth and success, Leslie Charteris faced some difficult times, and this was one of his reasons for his taking other jobs; but the Saint was gradually bringing him fame and fortune.

Now Leslie Charteris finds himself living the sort of existence every man dreams about – entirely his own master, with time and money to see the world and taste as many of the luxuries of life as those enjoyed by the Saint himself.

THE STICK MAN

The Saint is always associated with the simple but effective "stick man" emblem, a halo circling above his head. This emblem was created by Leslie Charteris who said, "I've been a writer all my life and I created the Saint "stick man" when I was about nine. I produced a magazine, writing everything in it – about four typed pages. It had everything, including a comic strip; but since I am no artist, all the characters were stick figures. How do you make a stick man into a Saint? You simply put a halo over his head!"

The Saint Leads a Dance

A grey haired, middle aged man was sitting on a bench in the park by the lake watching his beautiful wife and two children feed the ducks.

There were few people about because, although the sun was out and the day was bright, it was still a cold January day.

The man, Tomas Topal to his British friends, but Topalski in the land of his birth, had managed to escape from Eastern Europe and settle in England eighteen months ago. A brilliant scientist, he was welcomed by the Establishment and his exit was mourned by the government of his own country. He had expected to be followed and harassed by foreign agents but had been surprised when nothing was done to persuade him to return. Because he was immersed in his researches he gave little thought to his past life, living only for the present and the future.

His wife, Ludmia on the other hand was worried for fear of reprisals and fussed over her family like an old mother hen. It was in one of her rare unguarded moments, while she was talking to her children about the ducks, that a large car drove slowly up and stopped by the bridge. A thick-set man with an impassive face spoke in a low voice to the two seated at the back.

"You know what to do. See to it."

Quickly and silently the two men left the car. They stopped to make sure no-one was about, then swooped down on Topalski. His cry alerted Ludmia who let out a scream of terror as she saw her husband dragged towards the waiting car. She continued to scream until she saw the man in front take out his gun and deliberately aim at one of the children. Terrified she turned and fell over them protectively.

The men bundled Topalski into the back of the car; the car drove off at speed and when Ludmia looked up again it was nowhere in sight.

Ludmia ran and ran, holding a child by each hand. She was sobbing, the children were crying, but the few passers by hurried on, not wishing to become involved in anyone else's tragedy.

The Saint was coming home from France on the night ferry service. Rather a mundane way to travel for one so longing for adventure but flying had become so boring that Simon Templar had decided on a change. All sorts of things could happen on the water

between the French and English coast. This time was no exception.

He was on deck watching the waves frill out behind when he noticed a man in a scruffy mackintosh standing by the opposite rail. The Saint frowned. Something about the figure was familiar. The man half turned so that the Saint caught his profile. "My old friend Jimmy Forbes! Now what are you doing on this little tub?" he said to himself. He was just about to go over and speak to him when he saw another man sidle up and draw Forbes into conversation.

It took only a couple of minutes, then Forbes slumped to the ground and the man was gone.

The Saint ran over to Forbes who was lying on the deck with an eight inch knife in his chest. The Saint went to draw it out.

"Don't" gasped Forbes. "Done for."

"It's Simon Templar, old son, tell me . . ."

"Listen, for God's sake," croaked Forbes. "Tell Alistair, Cardia . . . the ballet . . . next." Forbes sank back to the deck and lost consciousness.

The Saint took off his coat and covered him up. He went to the rail and peered through the darkness but there was now no sign of Forbes' assailant. He went quickly to an officer and begged the use of a wheel chair for a friend who had been taken ill. Fortunately they were just about to dock so the staff were busy at their stations and the wheel chair was forthcoming with little questioning.

He put Forbes in it, sitting upright, collected his own things and wheeled his invalid up on deck. He was standing waiting to disembark when a knife whizzed through the air, grazed his left ear and became embedded in the woodwork behind him. He ran to the rails and looked down to see a skinny, dark man run to a car and get in. The car

The man raised his eyebrows. "Is he dead?" he asked nodding at Forbes.

"Yes," said the Saint.

"Then I think you'd better come along with me."

The Saint renewed his acquaintanceship with Alistair McInley in a small room in a side street off Whitehall. He had helped out with several assignments in the past, when he had been in the right spot at the right time and Alistair's men had been in a spot of bother.

Although the Department did not officially approve of the Saint or his methods, Alistair owed him several debts, one of which he repaid now by listening to every word the Saint said and believing him.

"Cardia . . . the ballet." Alistair repeated, tapping his front teeth with a white envelope.

The Saint broke in on Alistair's reverie. "Are you going to fill me in? I'd like to help. Forbes was a good man."

"Of course. Forbes was on to a traffic in human life."

"Which way?" asked the Saint.

"From us to them," said Alistair.

"Defectors?" asked the Saint.

"Let's say they were people who preferred to live here than there. Nothing political, mainly artists, writers, the last one was a scientist. Unfortunately for him Jimmy's message didn't reach us until it was too late."

"How come?"

"Jimmy's contact worked in Adrian's, the hairdressers in Bond Street. Jimmy would leave a message with Max, his contact, and he would pass the word to us. The day Jimmy went in Max was away with flu. He asked one of the other assistants to telephone Max at his home number with a name, but the assistant forgot until the next day."

drove quickly off. It carried a diplomatic immunity badge which made the Saint smile cynically.

While he was still looking at the car he saw another figure standing at the foot of the gangplank. "And you're not going to be too pleased at the turn of events," the Saint said softly.

He wheeled Forbes down the gangplank and stopped by this man. "You looking for him?" he asked.

The man gazed at him stony faced.

"If you're from MI5"

"I've got to talk to Alistair. Forbes gave me a message." the Saint said quietly.

The man still looked coldly at the Saint.

"Simon Templar," said the Saint. "Do you want my card?"

"Conveniently do you think?" asked the Saint.

"Could be, but we have no way of telling."

"I think I'll pay a visit to Mr. Adrian's establishment."

"Go carefully, we don't want to blow his cover," Alistair advised him. "But Cardia . . . the ballet . . . puzzling that!" He picked up the telephone and dialled three digits. "Jerry, have we anyone on the staff who's keen on ballet?"

There was a silence while Alistair listened. "Send her up here now will you?"

Two minutes later a young secretary knocked and came into the room.

"Sit down my dear. You're a keen ballet fan. Would the name Cardia mean anything to you?"

She thought for a moment. "Lovely dancer, going to be a great star. Been here three years. Calls himself John Marks now. He's dancing Coppelia tonight."

"Thank you my dear. I can see we've trained you well." Alistair chuckled as the girl left the room.

"So what happens now?" asked the Saint.

"We'll arrange for a round-the-clock watch to be kept on him."

"Right. I'm off to have a hair cut."

"Keep in touch. And remember they're a rough, tough outfit."

The Saint went home to his Mews house and had a bath and some breakfast. Then he put on his newest suit, selected the most bizarre tie he owned and took a taxi to Adrians in Bond Street.

The hairdresser's windows were tinted so that from the outside you could only see outlines of customers. Inside the decor was ultra modern and there was loud rock music coming from the stereo speakers. All the customers were young having freaky hair styles bestowed upon them by stylists who were no older than themselves.

Having told the receptionist he had been recommended and would like Max to style his hair, he was ushered up to the end of the salon and a good looking young Slav handed him a nylon coat.

"Jimmy Forbes sent me," said the Saint.

Max turned a pale shade of grey. "You shouldn't have come," he whispered. "I think they're on to me. Now how would you like it done?" He clipped away with the scissors.

"Steady," warned the Saint.

"I've got to make it look right," Max told him.

The Saint looked in the mirror to see the result and noticed the skinny man from the dock coming through the door of the shop. "Put a towel over my face," he ordered quickly.

Max did what he was told. "A massage is just what you need." He said professionally.

After the Saint went to the desk to pay his bill, he walked to the door.

"Your coat sir," said a voice.

"I didn't have . . ." but before he finished his sentence he was pinioned from behind and dragged down some stairs at the back. Here he came face to face with the skinny man.

"That's him. I'd know him anywhere."

A thick set man with an impassive face said in a low voice. "Tie him up and put him out."

"And Max?"

"You know what to do," said the voice,

which was the last thing the Saint heard before a pad of evil smelling cotton wool was held firmly against his face.

He came to in semi darkness. He was still in the basement of the shop and the street lights of Bond Street were filtering through the glass leaded lights in the pavement above. He had a splitting headache and both his hands and feet were tied.

He sat up and began to tug with his teeth at the handkerchief in his top pocket. As the handerchief came up so did his penknife with it. He caught the knife and opened it with his teeth. Holding the knife behind he gradually sawed at the ropes that tied his hands. Once these were free he was able to deal with the ropes that tied his feet.

He made his way up to the empty shop, through to the back and up some stairs to a private office. He heard a low voice giving orders over the telephone. "You will stand by as arranged. I will be down with the truck. Josef will be picking up Cardia after the performance tonight. We have had to change our plans and act sooner than we planned. Be ready to sail as soon as we arrive."

The Saint ran lightly down the stairs. He hailed a taxi and told the driver "Covent Garden".

Once there he telephoned Alistair from the pub across the road. "It's tonight Alistair. They're going to take him by truck to the coast and then by sea."

"Good. I'll get my men to stop them."

"No. Let them go ahead with their plan."

"Good Heavens, man, do you know what you're saying?"

"Of course. But they won't get him because I'm going to take his place."

"You're not suggesting you dance Coppelia."

"No. But you're going to get me carte blanche to be at the side of the stage so we can switch once the performance is over."

"It's too great a risk. I can't allow it."

"But you want to catch the operators at the other end don't you. Otherwise they can still carry on with their human traffic."

"Right. Give me time to contact one of my men, then he can give you his two way radio. Keep in touch. Let me know where you're heading. You might need help the other end."

If the Saint hadn't had work to do he
might have been fascinated with the
inner workings of the Opera House; he
might even have noticed how many
beautiful young dancers there were.
Instead he watched the male dancer like
a hawk and at the end, he bundled him
into a laundry basket and away to another
part of the building.

Then he went to the star's dressing
room, put on Cardia's coat and hat and
emerged from the door, only to be seized
by two men and dragged along a narrow
corridor.

Pressing a revolver in his back one of
the men said, "Make a sound and you're

dead. Walk out naturally and say goodnight as usual."

The Saint did what he was told. He was walked out into the street and along the road where a truck was waiting. Doors were opened and he was bundled in to it. The two men slammed the doors and the truck drove off.

The Saint took out his radio and sent a message to Alistair.

"O.K. We've got you covered," was his reassuring answer and the Saint settled down for a long trip.

After they had been travelling for about an hour his radio bleeped. "You're heading down the estuary and you've got plenty of back up if you need it."

Later the truck stopped. The doors were flung open and the Saint was dragged out.

"Careful," said the low voice to the men who were manhandling him. "Don't hurt him. They can do that at the other end." The sentence was finished with a sadistic laugh.

The two men marched him down to the water's edge. The Saint put up a minimal struggle but the men had him firmly in their grasp.

Suddenly there was a commotion behind.

"Look the cops have got the truck. Quick, get this guy on board, or we've had it."

They dragged a protesting Saint on board. "Cast off – get on with it," yelled one of the men.

The pilot set the boat in motion. The Saint waited patiently.

"You stay here," said one man. "I'll take him below and give him a shot." He pushed the Saint in the back and followed.

The Saint walked down the steps slowly and as they reached the bottom he turned and hit the man full in the face. He grunted and fell like a sack to the ground.

"Nice work," called the man on top thinking it was the Saint who had collapsed. "Come and enjoy the air."

The Saint climbed the steps. The man had his back to him. Three paces was all that was needed and a karate chop to the man's neck. Then the Saint tipped him overboard.

Next he made his way to the pilot's cabin. "Everything O.K.?" asked the pilot, not turning as the door opened.

The Saint held a revolver in his back. "Everything certainly is O.K. Now you just do what you're told, mon ami. Carry on as if nothing had happened."

The boat sped through the water to its destination. Near the French coast a light signalled three times. "Give your answer," ordered the Saint pressing the gun further into the pilot's ribs. "Now what happens?"

"He comes out in a dinghy, picks up the passenger and I go back alone."

"Right. One word out of place and I'll blow you to Kingdom Come."

They waited in silence, while a dinghy approached. The boat came alongside and a man clambered aboard. "One parcel to collect, Patrick. All nicely tied up I hope." He came through the door and the Saint gave him an uppercut worthy of a champion.

"Now," he said pointing the gun at Patrick. "Home James at the double."

A few days later the Saint was invited to Covent Garden by Cardia, or John Marks, who was at the bar limbering up. "I hear I owe you my life. Perhaps you'd better try this step in case you have to impersonate me again."

The Saint went to the bar and tried. "Hells Bells!" he cried and held his back in pain. "Each to his own. I think I'll stick to crime."

THE SAINT DRIVES A JAGUAR

XK120 Roadster

SS 100 Two Seater Sports

The Saint's choice of car was influenced by the superb racing pedigree of Jaguar. Jaguar, a name that has become so famous and so evocative of success, speed and style, that the original meaning of the word "a lithe and beautiful animal of the cat family" is probably lost to many of those who now buy the car. *Jaguar*, meaning car, has almost taken over from *Jaguar* meaning cat in the English language.

The story in fact started in 1922 with the Swallow Sidecar Company, which produced sidecars for motorcycles. In 1927 the first motorcar introduced was the Swallow Austin two seater with a 747 cc engine. The car cost £174.

It was not until 1935 that the name *Jaguar* was used. The SS Jaguar 1½ litre s.v. saloon and the SS Jaguar 2½ litre o.h.v. saloon and tourer were introduced along with famous SS 100 two seater sports (2663 cc), still praised as one of the best cars of its era, (1). In September 1938 the 3½ litre car turned in a best one-way speed of 101.12 m.p.h.

In 1948 the XK120 open two seater was introduced the first of a long line of "modern sports cars". In 1949 a White XK120 roadster clocked a flying mile at 132.596 m.p.h. At the same time as the XK120, Jaguar introduced the MK V saloon car.

The "C" type Jaguars were purpose-built sports racing cars which were lighter and better than the XK120. In 1951 the "C" type Jaguar won the Le Mans Race and in 1953 they took first, second and fourth places also at Le Mans.

The "D" type Jaguar was introduced in 1954 specifically to win the Le Mans Race, which it did in 1955, 1956 and in 1957, they came first, second, third, fourth and sixth, a tremendous achievement.

Bred on the racing circuit, it was the Jaguar produced cars which became a familiar and envied sight on the roads of Britain. In 1954 the XK120 was superseded by the XK140 and in 1957 saw the introduction of the XK150. This was to be the last of the

The Racing 'D' Type Jaguar

XK150 Drophead Coupe

"E" Type Series 1 Fixed Head Coupe

"E" Type Series 3 V12 Roadster

Simon Templar's XJS

XK Series for the time being for in 1961 the world famous Jaguar "E" Type was announced. This car had a maximum speed of 150 m.p.h. with a 3.8 litre engine. In 1964 a larger engine was introduced (4.2 litres) "E" Type Series 2 and in 1968 an "E" Type series II appeared on the market. Following this, in 1971 the beautiful V12 "E" Type was introduced (5343 cc) using a larger. smoother engine in the Jaguar "E" Type body.

In recent years Jaguar concentrated on the production of its sophisticated, saloon cars, the XJ12 and XJ6, but in 1975 introduced the car which is now the pride of its owner "Simon Templar", the XJ-S. This car has a 5443cc engine and all the sophisticated power and comfort of a vehicle required by those who need to travel fast and safely.

Simon Templar drives a Jaguar XJ-S, Number Plate ST1, with the assurance that the car he is driving has been born and bred through many years of racing competition. He knows that Jaguars have been driven by some of the world's great drivers, Duncan Hamilton, Mike Hawthorn, Denis Hulme, Roy Salvadori and Stirling Moss.

All You Need is a Good Agent....

58

THE SAINT AT HOME

Simon Templar, otherwise known as the Saint, is not the sort of man to be content with a suburban semi-detached.

His London home is just what you'd expect. A luxurious pad, if ever there was one, as viewers will soon discover when seeing Ian Ogilvy portraying Templar in the "RETURN OF THE SAINT" series.

So we accepted Ian Ogilvy's invitation to his mews flat in Mayfair, to see what designer John Stoll had created for him – and if you happened to be a member of the female sex, you might well wonder what lies up that white-painted wrought iron spiral staircase should the invitation extend to climbing it (quite clearly to bedroom and bathroom but, to one's disillusionment on the set, petering out as it reaches the first tier of studio lamps!).

Taking care to avoid tripping on the two stairs from the front door which lead straight into the living-room, one's eye stretches around the commodious appartment and straight across to the raised level dining annex.

The apartment is wall-to-wall carpeted throughout in grey, with loose white sheepskin carpets for extra comfort, easy chairs, glass-topped tables plus a music centre. The walls are brown.

Up two steps into the dining annex, walls beige-tinted, light streaming in through French windows, tubular chairs around a large circular glass dining table. Through the wide opening on one side can be seen the Kitchen – ultra modern with all the gadgets to make life easy for a bachelor like the Saint.

The sort of pad, which has elegance, and taste – no surprise from the Saint.

ANSWERS

THE SAINT

1. James Bond is the character that **Roger Moore** is now more well known as.

2. The author of the original Saint books is **Leslie Charteris.**

3. Todays Simon Templar drives a **Jaguar XJS.**

4. You should have got this one, it's on the cover after all – **Ian Ogilvy.**

CROSSWORD

ACROSS

1. Sell
2. Ball
4. Crash
6. Ring
7. Aim
10. Simon
11. Templar
12. Tea
13. Rung
14. Neck
16. Hot
18. Rope
20. Air
21. Cry
23. Pair
24. Dinner
26. Share
28. Ash
29. Hope
31. Crawl
32. Comb
33. Hate
35. Beat
37. Break
38. Bait
39. Tool
40. Link

DOWN

1. Smoke
2. Ban
3. Can
4. Crime
5. Hair
8. Mail
9. Jaguar
10. Saint
11. Thief
15. City
16. Happy
17. Hard
19. Pearls
22. Respectable
23. Pare
25. Nail
27. Trouble
30. Open
34. Think
36. Sail

ROUND THE WORLD

1. The leaning tower is in Pisa, Italy.

2. Washington, not New York, is the capital of the United States.

3. The French underground railway is called the Metro.

4. Venice is the city with no cars or roads, it has a system of canals.

5. Mount Fuji is in Japan.

6. Hong Kong is the place for rickshaws.

7. Finland is known as the land of the midnight sun.

8. Omsk is in Russia.

9. Birds nest soup is a delicacy in China.

10. Aborigines are the natives of Australia.